10 YEARS OF

'Believe me, if you'd met
my son you'd be against
hereditary peerages'

The Daily Telegraph

10 YEARS OF

'Sorry I'm late. My train arrived on time, I fainted and missed it'

ORION

Orion Books
A division of the Orion Publishing Group Ltd
Orion House
5 Upper St Martin's Lane
London
WC2H 9EA

This collected edition first published by
Orion Books Ltd in 2001

Second impression 2001

A CIP catalogue record for this book is available
from the British Library.

ISBN 0 75284 472 5

Printed and bound in Great Britain by
Butler & Tanner Ltd, Frome and London

'I hope I have a better Thursday
than I did yesterday'

Foreword
Ten of the Best – Matt's Choice

This is the first ever cartoon of mine to appear on the front page of the *Telegraph*. I was still a waiter at the time and I was in the office just to drop off a cartoon for the City Diary when I was told that Max Hastings, the editor, was writing a piece apologising that the wrong date had been printed on that day's paper; Thursday 25 February 1988 had come a day too early. Confused readers had been ringing to say they'd been turning up for the wrong appointments and having rows in the Post Office.

This was my big break, and from then on I concentrated full time on cartooning. There's a couple in the Blackheath Pizza Express who are still waiting for two coffees and their bill.

At the office my desk is in the graphics department. One day the designer sitting next to me was drawing a map of the proposed Chunnel link route. I watched as he drew a dotted line through the street and under the house I had just bought in south east London.

I decided to think of a cartoon first, and kill myself later.

'Come on, move along now, there's nothing to see'

There's always a danger that a cartoon will be overtaken by events. So on the night of the 1997 election result I left the newspaper with three cartoons to cover every possible outcome:

a) Tories lose
b) Tories lose badly
c) Disaster for Tories

The disaster version was used in all editions.

'I'm worried it might crash when we go from BC to AD'

A lot of people suspected that the dangers of the millennium bug were being exaggerated by computer analysts trying to make a fast buck. In fact the whole thing was invented by cartoonists looking for a subject to make jokes about.

'Typical! You wait 25 years
for a ceasefire and then
suddenly two come along'

Every morning I sit down in front
of an A2 layout pad and write
down all the subjects in the day's
news. I then try to think of as
many jokes on each one as I can.

This is the only one I've ever
managed to come up with about
Northern Ireland.

*'It's from the Social Services.
They're going to send you
on a safari'*

People often say, somewhat harshly, that cartooning is just putting together two news stories. Although this is true, it's not as simple as it looks and could be dangerous if attempted by members of the public who are not professionally trained cartoonists.

The two stories on the day of this cartoon were: 'Juvenile Criminals Sent On Exotic Holidays' and 'Lions Attack Zoo Visitor'.

'I'm afraid your car failed the
tough new emissions test,
but it did get six GCSEs'

I usually have a pretty good idea which cartoons are likely to offend the readers, but the fact that this one upset a couple of people took me by surprise. They were hurt by the suggestion that exams were getting too easy.

Personally, I've always been overjoyed to pass any exam, however simple.

John Major was having a particularly difficult time as Prime Minister when I did this cartoon. I didn't think he'd enjoy it, but he sent me a charming letter saying how much it made him laugh.

In a disgraceful act of cartoonist sleaze I sent him the original.

THIS IS AN EMERGENCY
CARTOON. SINCE THE
BOMB SCARE MATT
HAS BEEN UNDER
HIS DESK.

One day in November 1992 a
special 'emergency edition' of the
Daily Telegraph appeared with a
blank front page, because the
building had to be evacuated after
an IRA bomb scare. The next day
I produced this. It may not be my
funniest cartoon, but it was certainly
the easiest to draw.

Cartoons without captions are always popular. This one, on the inaccuracy of NATO's bombing in the war in Kosovo, is one of my favourites.

10 YEARS OF

'They're waiting for the price to drop by another couple of thousand'

1991

The Sporting Life

'Would you rather watch
the rain at Wimbledon or
the rain at Lords?'

'You didn't let him
watch the McEnroe
match, did you?'

The Sporting Life

'Well, that's the first setback for the England team'

'The England cricket team are coming in . . . They'll probably be out again in a few minutes?'

The Sporting Life

'It looks as if the England fans
have been here as well'

'Paul Gascoigne's gone. I sold
him to an Italian police
station for £4 million'

Hard Times

'I've bn mde rdndnt'

'This used to be a really nice
Jobcentre until the middle
classes moved in'

Hard Times

'This is a hold-up. Move slowly towards the till and buy something'

Talking of Politics

'I didn't sleep a wink. I'm so
excited about the
Citizen's Charter'

'If a poll tax form has your
name on it, there's nothing
you can do about it'

Talking of Politics

'We've spotted a Liberal Democrat – they're extremely rare'

'I haven't got the heart to send Mrs Thatcher her poll tax rebate'

The Modern Military

'A delicious contribution
to the war effort from the
Belgians, eh Sarge?'

'Look, he's coming out
of the closet'

Law and Order

'We've reason to believe you've been using a hose-pipe on this beanstalk, Jack'

MY OTHER CAR IS BEING STOLEN

Law and Order

'Oh dear, I can't remember
if I locked my back door'

Transport Troubles

'Darling, your season ticket has arrived'

'Did you have a good day at the railway station, dear?'

Transport Troubles

'I can hear a government subsidy but I don't think it's coming this way'

'Apparently the British have 37 different words for BR'

The Nation's Health

'I've run out of newspaper –
I'll wrap them in a
Government healthy diet
report instead'

'Could you make me just
a bit better for £2?'

It's A Funny Old World

'It's the recession'

'We traded in the Fiesta –
this needs no petrol and
hardly any water'

It's A Funny Old World

'I can't remember the exact
date of birth, but I know
petrol was £2.27'

'And don't tell people you
work for a petrol company
– pretend you're a
poll tax collector'

It's A Funny Old World

'I don't think this counts as
swimming the Channel, sir'

'Look, there's that nice
couple we met here last
bank holiday'

It's A Funny Old World

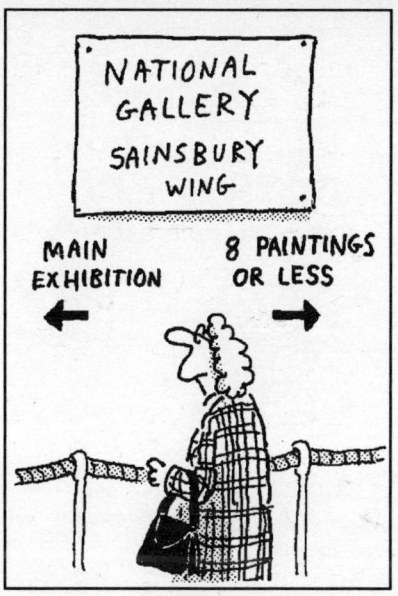

'He's captured brilliantly
the lack of facilities,
transport and cheap
housing in rural areas'

It's A Funny Old World

MODEL
MISSOURI

'I suppose you'll be free to go shopping on Sundays now you're retiring, Dr Runcie'

It's A Funny Old World

'Type yourself a letter of apology for what I did at the office party last night'

'I'm not doing the test for seven-year-olds – I'm at the Primary School of Life'

1992

School's Out

'We're the three wise men'

'We've had an attractive trans-
fer offer for you from a school
lower down the league'

School's Out

'Good news — I've bottomed out'

'I'm so worried by the new tests I can't concentrate on being a tree swaying in the wind'

Hard Times

'It's a marvel of evolution –
an out-of-worker bee'

'I must say it's nice to see
more women in senior
positions in business'

Hard Times

'I'm afraid I'm going to have
to ask you to leave'

'That was the day I popped
out and bought a sandwich'

Hard Times

'I'm interested in obtaining one of these imprudent loans'

Talking of Politics

'You're not going to put me down as a margin of error, are you?'

'Are you being fattened up for privatisation, grandad?'

Talking of Politics

'Oh shut up about having a say'

'Under the Citizen's Charter they have to keep us better informed'

Talking of Politics

'Party political broadcast on the NHS – Take Nine'

'Don't think of it as refusing to sign a treaty, think of it as conserving ink'

Talking of Politics

'If Labour gets in we could
cancel out our losses by
having 25 children'

'I don't know how I'll
vote – I leave all that
to my accountant'

Talking of Politics

'I may be overdrawn, but I'm expecting an electoral bribe very shortly'

'Maybe the person who valued my house would like to buy it'

The Modern Military

'. . . and what's going to happen to our regimental mascot?'

'A lot of the pageantry has gone since the defence cuts'

Law and Order

'I want you to get up to about 100 mph, pull on the handbrake, spin the vehicle and hit the horn'

'Oh brilliant. I'm released just as the whole prison service is about to be reformed'

Transport Troubles

'I'd like to buy a ticket, but not all at once'

'This train has always been called the 8.57, but nobody can remember why'

The Nation's Health

'Would you like to spit?'

'I hear you now control your own budget, doctor'

The Sporting Life

'I haven't got the heart to tell them this isn't the Wimbledon queue'

TABLE SOCCER VIOLENCE

The Sporting Life

'Could you slow down
occasionally so people get
a chance to read our logos?'

The Sporting Life

'It's a combination of the new superbike and the Spanish tummy bug'

'Have you ever wondered
why we have webbed feet?'

It's A Funny Old World

'Let's use the toaster for now and we'll try nuclear fusion again tomorrow'

It's A Funny Old World

'The vicar's trying to compete with the Sunday-opening supermarkets'

'Psst, there's someone at the finishing line who's interested in buying your house'

It's A Funny Old World

'Unplaced at Crufts again?'

'I've always wanted a
box at the opera'

1993

Talking of Politics

'We watch Red Hot Dutch every evening—it's the only channel where they never mention Maastricht'

'If I hadn't got out a copy of the Maastricht treaty they would never have left'

Talking of Politics

'I can't help wondering how they'll vote in the referendum'

2,000 BEDS TO GO

Talking of Politics

'I didn't tell Mrs Rimington
she was invited—I assumed
she'd find out'

'I'm only pollinating deserv-
ing flowers that are married'

Hard Times

'We'll never get a taxi. Let's just buy one of these houses'

'That's an encouraging sign of an upturn in retail sales'

Hard Times

'Wait there—we're coming
up to join you'

Hard Times

'Call me an old softie, but I've given in to Mr Major's plea to limit your pay rise'

'It's not a nicotine patch, it's my bank statement—it reminds me I can't afford to smoke'

Law and Order

'And this is the current
Marquess of Blandford'

Law and Order

'Police? Can you see with your High Street video camera if the greengrocer has any broccoli?'

'The judge called me a vigilante and gave me six months'

Law and Order

'I now declare this juvenile secure unit open'

'It's very sad—this used to be a tyre and exhaust centre before all the car thefts'

Law and Order

'I wouldn't know about that—someone stole my watch'

'You treat this place like a privatised prison'

The Sporting Life

'I cut myself shaving'

'Your jockey is in danger
of exceeding the 48-hour
working week'

It's A Funny Old World

'We're rich—I've lost
my driver's licence'

'That's not a button,
it's a hard ecu'

It's A Funny Old World

'If we wish upon a star
maybe all our dreams
will come true'

THIS IS AN EMERGENCY
CARTOON. SINCE THE
BOMB SCARE MATT
HAS BEEN UNDER
HIS DESK.

It's A Funny Old World

'I'm afraid you're too late'

'How marvellous, a woman up Everest—now she can tidy the place up a bit'

It's A Funny Old World

'I heard an oil tanker's run aground. I wonder if it's us'

It's A Funny Old World

'Do you have the feeling that other people are answering more sex surveys than you?'

'I'm living out one of my fantasies'

It's A Funny Old World

'How far back do you think
you dropped your wallet?'

1994

The Nation's Health

'And when the music stops...'

'Would you mind if some students watch this?'

The Nation's Health

'Take me to a hospital that's
higher up the league table'

Hard Times

'I've come to read the
Appointments Section of
your newspaper'

'DON'T JUMP!'

Law and Order

'There was going to be a
riot here as well,
but we overslept'

The Sporting Life

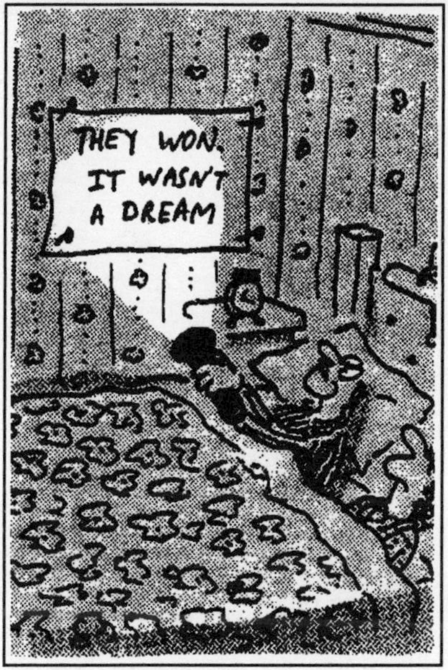
THEY WON. IT WASN'T A DREAM

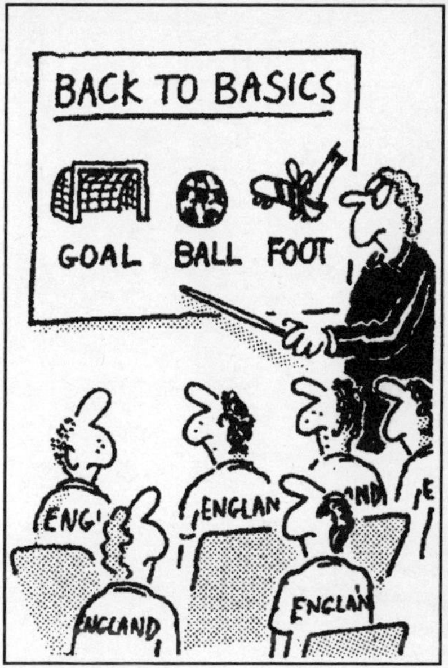
BACK TO BASICS
GOAL
BALL
FOOT

School's Out

'I wanted to go to the new
lesson on responsible sex but
I couldn't get a baby-sitter'

Transport Troubles

'Passengers waiting for the
13.22 are advised to use
a high factor sun cream'

'You'll be perfectly safe here'

Weather or Not

'Turned out dangerous again'

'If you're going to the
High Street stay
in the shallow end'

Weather or Not

'So, how long have you lived here in Sussex?'

'They come back to the same street every year to spawn'

It's A Funny Old World

'The electricians' union will
be coming back, but they
can't give us a definite time'

It's A Funny Old World

'Let's just say we encourage our employees to work on Sundays'

'. . . And please let the supermarket have an iceberg lettuce left'

It's A Funny Old World

'If I'm supplying the drink for your wedding I'd like to see you in here more often on Sundays'

It's A Funny Old World

'It was a million to one chance. He was run over by a British car'

'Unfortunately it's still our policy to buy British'

It's A Funny Old World

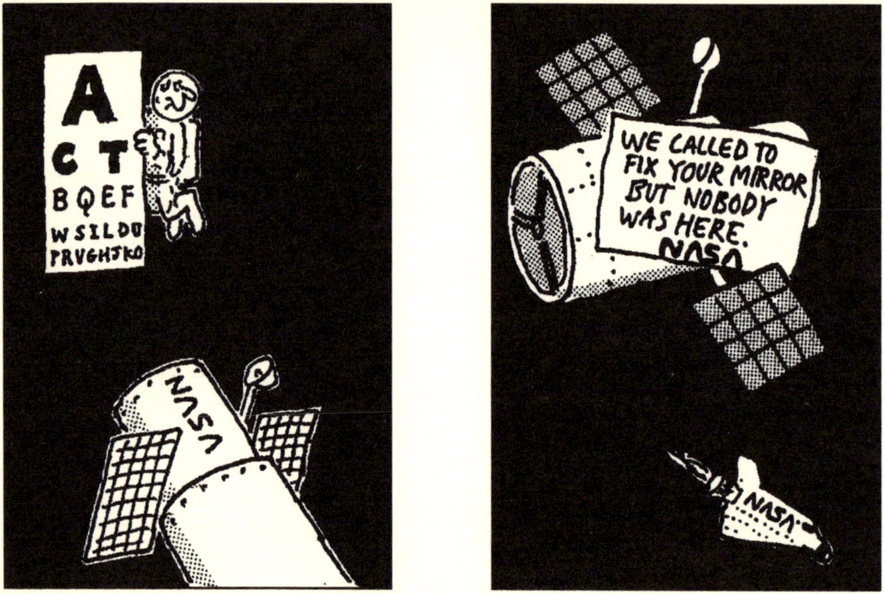
A
C T
B Q E F
WE CALLED TO FIX YOUR MIRROR BUT NOBODY WAS HERE. NASA

It's A Funny Old World

'Er . . . sorry, no. I'm saving
myself for the right survey'

'I'm afraid the arms industry
has become briefly entangled
with financial aid'

It's A Funny Old World

'I've seen a blurred photo of a visitor at EuroDisney but I think it's a fake'

'Will it open before EuroDisney closes?'

It's A Funny Old World

'In London every £10 note has been through a water company's accounts at least five times'

'It was the Child Support Agency that told me to eat my husband'

1995

Talking of Politics

'No, not victory—that's
how many votes I got'

Talking of Politics

'My hiccups completely
vanished after that man
said he intended to vote
Conservative at the
next election'

'Typical! You wait 25 years
for a ceasefire and then
suddenly two come along'

Talking of Politics

'It's not my fault — God gave me sleaze genes'

'Now they can come and go as they please'

The Nation's Health

'Let's play doctors and nurses – I'll report you for incompetence'

'Say Aaaaaaarrrgggh'

Hard Times

'Miss Robins, jump out of the window for me, please'

'I suppose I should have seen this coming'

Hard Times

'I bought these on Saturday but I now realise I was coming out of recession too fast'

Law and Order

'No, my husband's in prison – he could walk in here at any moment'

'Being in Parkhurst is no excuse for not visiting your mother'

Law and Order

'How long do you intend to stay, sir?'

Law and Order

'I remember when you could leave your front door open and expect something to be stolen'

Law and Order

'By the way – I'm holding
Mr Jones in our broom
cupboard for questioning'

'I'm arresting you for
impersonating a member
of the Citizens' Patrol'

The Modern Military

'Who goes there — just a good friend, or foe?'

'On second thoughts, just shake my hand, Hardy'

The Sporting Life

'It's football practice
tomorrow so bring a
briefcase full of cash'

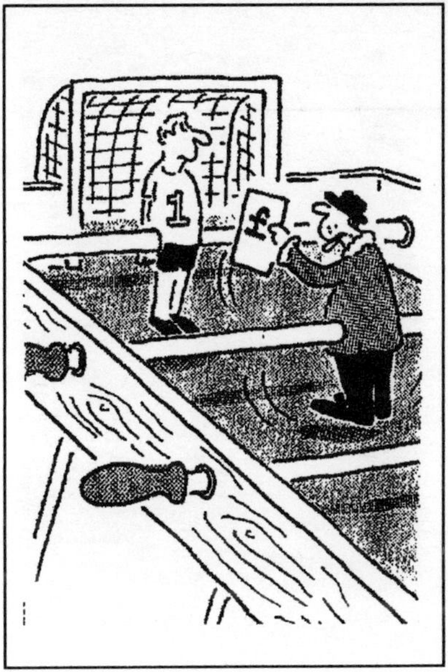
£
1

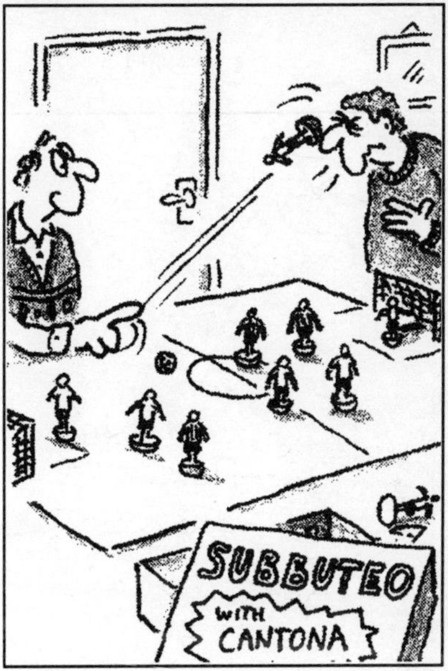
SUBBUTEO
WITH
CANTONA

It's A Funny Old World

'It's from the Social Services.
They're going to send you
on a safari'

'One . . . two . . . three . . .'

It's A Funny Old World

'Oh no, I've got a
Spanish fish finger'

It's A Funny Old World

'Do you have this in my size?
And how much do I get
for asking?'

It's A Funny Old World

'I put cucumber slices on my eyes to stop me reading any upsetting reports'

'He's not stuck, he's protesting against the M65'

1996

The Beef Crisis

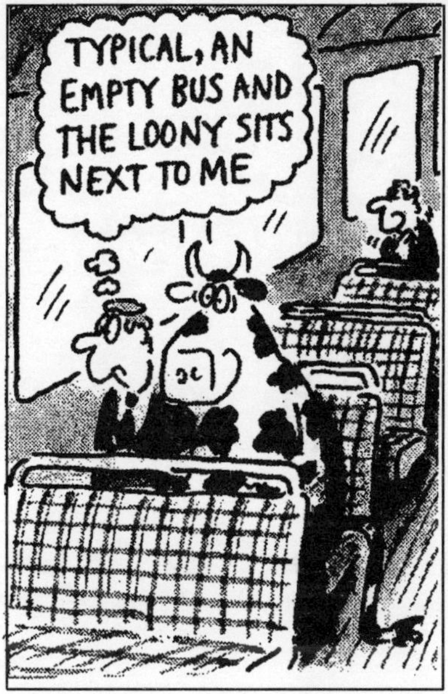
TYPICAL, AN EMPTY BUS AND THE LOONY SITS NEXT TO ME

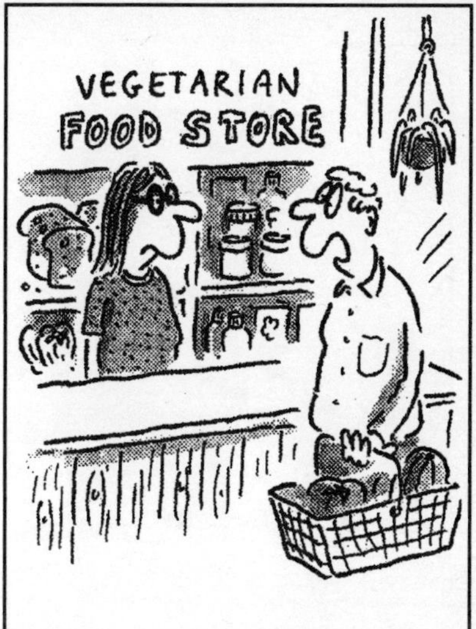
VEGETARIAN
FOOD STORE

'How nutty is the cutlet?'

The Beef Crisis

'I'm trying to start a
Mad Turkey Disease scare'

Talking of Politics

'I'm going to be spending more time with my butler'

Talking of Politics

'I told my wife I was working late at the office and she reported me to the EC'

Talking of Politics

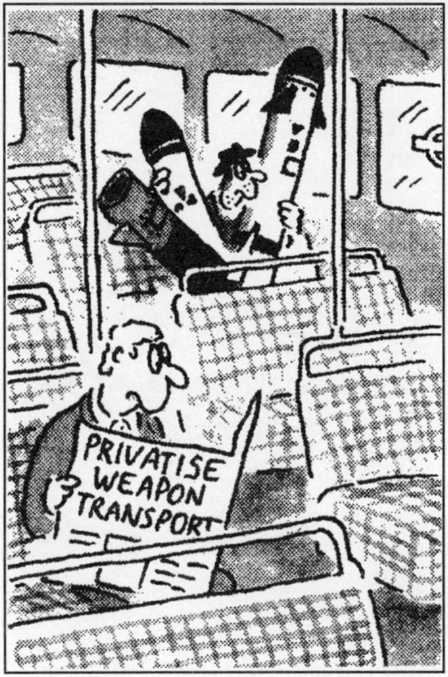
PRIVATISE WEAPON TRANSPORT

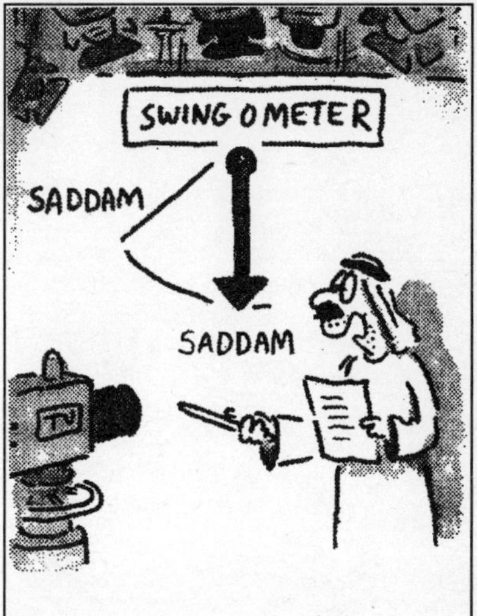
SWING O METER
SADDAM
SADDAM
TV

'Welcome to Iraqi Election Night Special'

Law and Order

'This is a warning – there's
a wobbly paving stone
right in front of you'

The Sporting Life

'Play is suspended for 25 years until global warming gives us the same climate as the Loire Valley'

'Sometimes it goes for as long as ten minutes without showing any sport'

The Sporting Life

'Put on the replay of the
Bruno, Tyson fight – I want
to time my boiled egg'

'I'll be Gascoigne, you
be Sheringham and our
jumpers can be the pub'

Weather or Not

'COME OUT, I know you're in there!'

It's A Funny Old World

'It's hard enough being black, but if they find out I'm gay...'

It's A Funny Old World

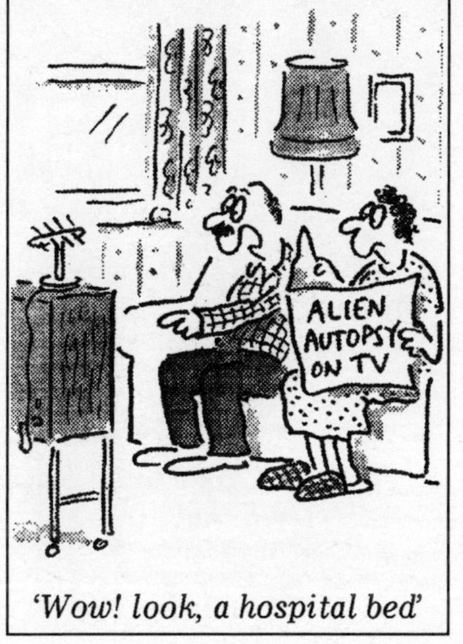
ALIEN
AUTOPSY
ON TV

'Wow! look, a hospital bed'

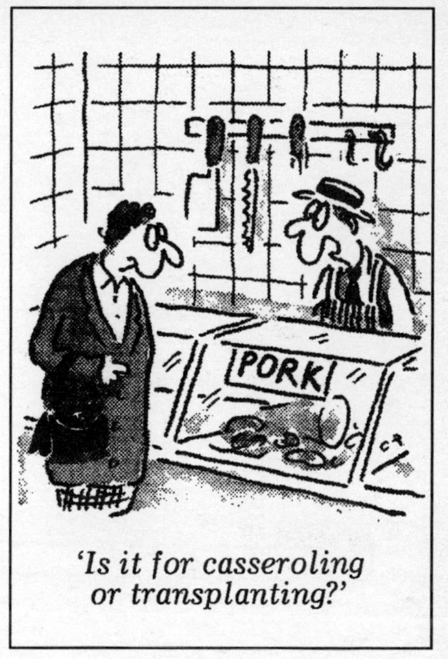
PORK

'Is it for casseroling or transplanting?'

It's A Funny Old World

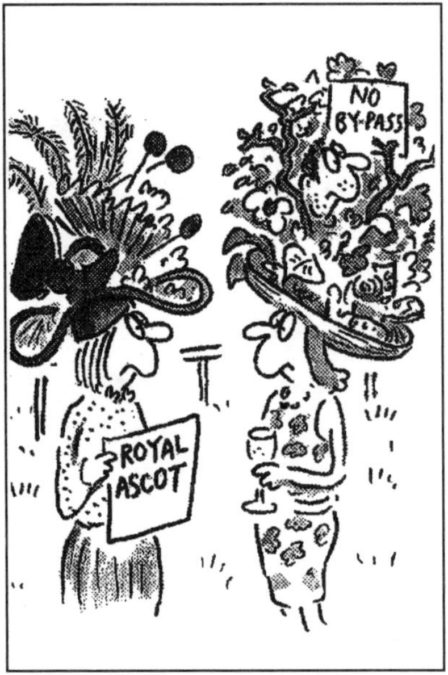
NO
BY-PASS
ROYAL
ASCOT

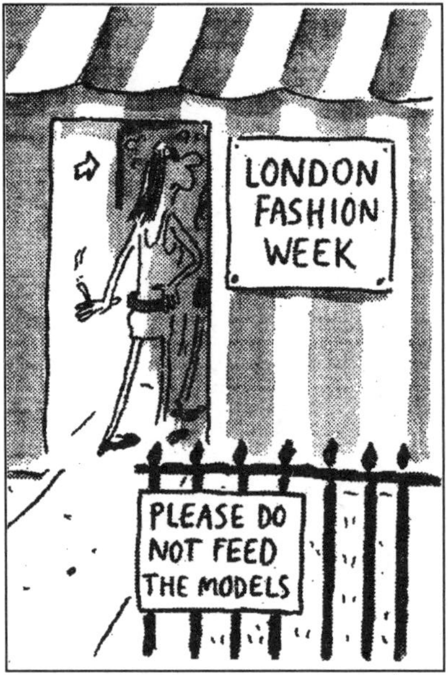
LONDON
FASHION
WEEK
PLEASE DO
NOT FEED
THE MODELS

It's A Funny Old World

'Is it too soon to send them a final demand?'

'YOU, yes <u>YOU</u>, Mr Robins, may have already <u>WON</u> the chance of <u>NOT</u> receiving ANY junk mail during the POST STRIKE!!!!!!!!!!!!!'

It's A Funny Old World

'We want one of
those old-fashioned
acrimonious divorces'

"The King feels that there
should be an element of
'fault' in divorce"

It's A Funny Old World

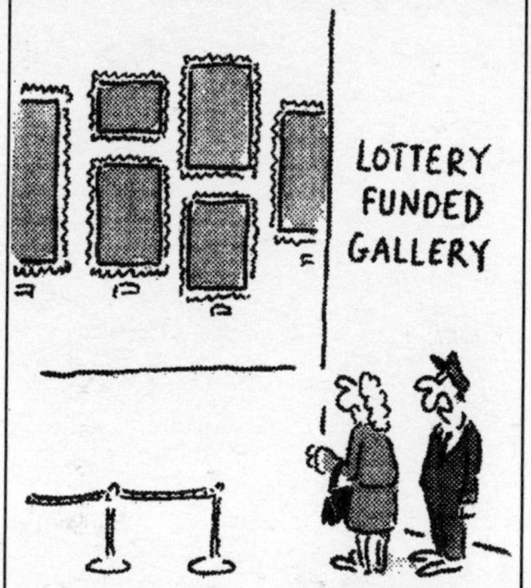
LOTTERY
FUNDED
GALLERY

'Scratch away the surface to reveal three Cezannes and win £50,000'

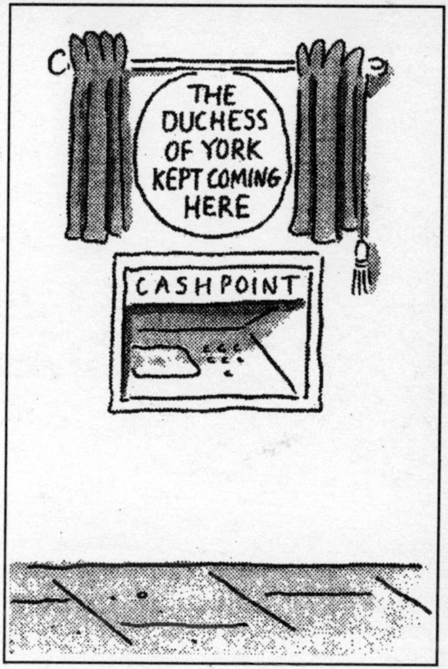
THE
DUCHESS
OF YORK
KEPT COMING
HERE
CASHPOINT

1997

Talking of Politics

'Your name has come up in our biscuits-for-tricks inquiry'

Talking of Politics

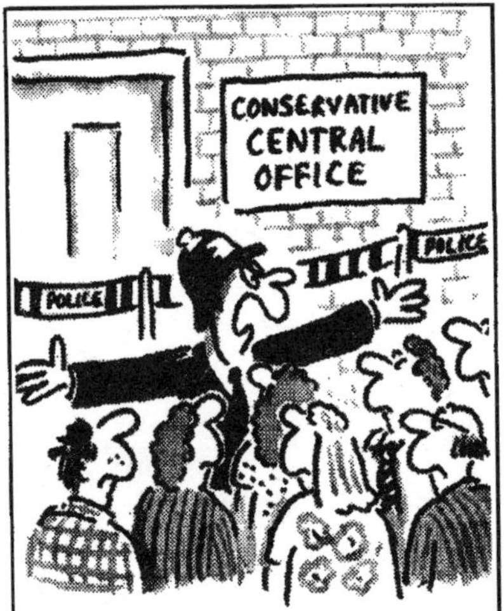
CONSERVATIVE
CENTRAL
OFFICE
POLICE
POLICE

'Come on, move along now, there's nothing to see'

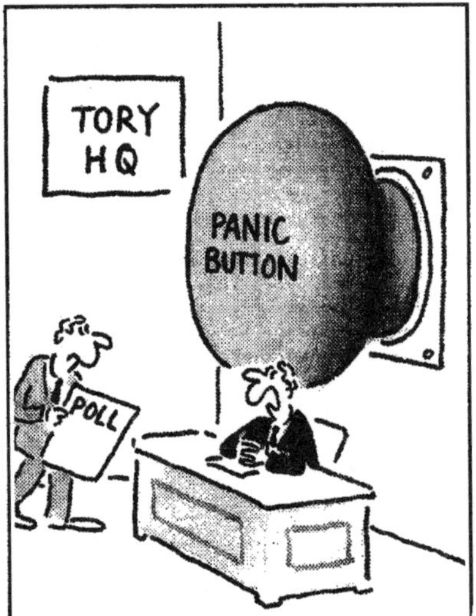
TORY
HQ
PANIC
BUTTON
POLL

'Now?'

Talking of Politics

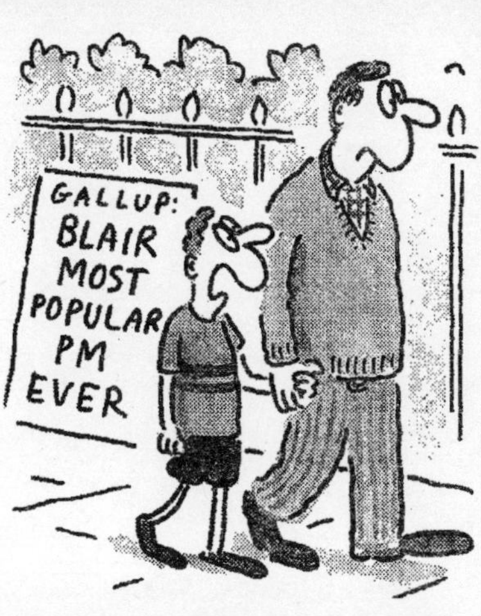
GALLUP:
BLAIR
MOST
POPULAR
PM
EVER

'Daddy, why does Tony Blair allow earthquakes to happen?'

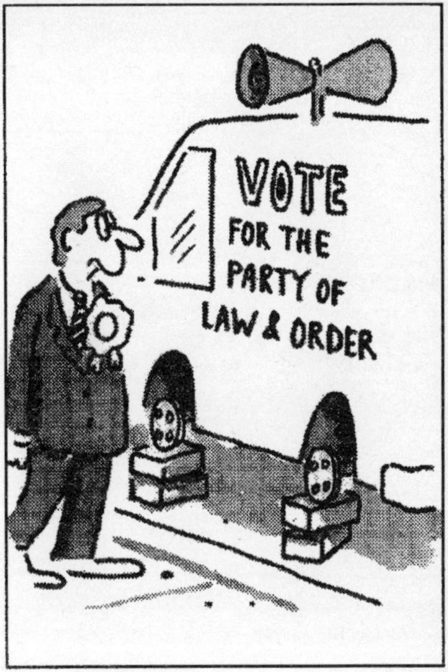
VOTE
FOR THE
PARTY OF
LAW & ORDER

Talking of Politics

'Jenkins, it looks like you'll
be getting my dinner in your
free time from now on'

'And we plan to pay for all
our spending commitments
with a windfall tax on the
Duchess of York'

Talking of Politics

'I feel uneasy – nothing dreadful has happened for 20 minutes'

'I had that Tory party in the back of my cab yesterday . . .'

Weather or Not

'Have you met my husband?
He's a weather forecaster'

School's Out

'I'm afraid your car failed the tough new emissions test, but it did get six GCSEs'

'Could you knock a bit off the tuition fees as I don't intend to go to many lectures?'

Religious Affairs

'I've been thinking of running away with a divorcee . . . hello . . . is anyone there?'

'Fortunately, our Catholic priest doesn't seem too interested in Labour's child benefit reforms'

The Nation's Health

'And that grey area there is your bed, which is what we'll be removing'

'Could you hide those cigarettes inside a copy of Gay News?'

The Nation's Health

'I'm going to quit smoking – I'm worried I'll get skin cancer standing out here'

The Nation's Health

'I gave up smoking after I was shown an X-ray of my wallet'

'Scalpel, swab, apple sauce...'

The Nation's Health

'He threw himself
downstairs just so he
could meet women'

It's A Funny Old World

I'm sorry M'lud, it's just something I feel very strongly about

'And Damien Hirst did the tail fin on this one'

It's A Funny Old World

'Isn't that the nice couple we had a near miss with last year?'

It's A Funny Old World

'That's left a nasty taste
in my mouth'

It's A Funny Old World

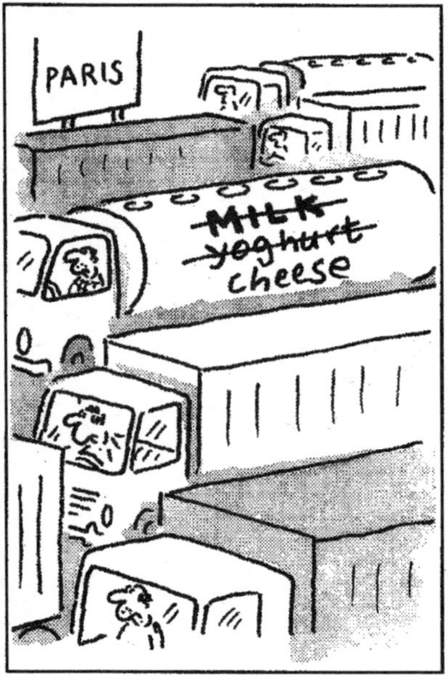
PARIS
MILK
yoghurt
cheese

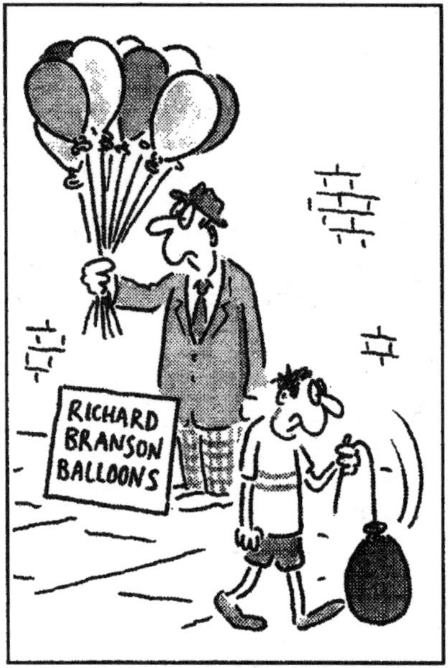
RICHARD BRANSON BALLOONS

It's A Funny Old World

'Hi, honey, I'm cloned'

'Scientists have discovered a link between not eating your greens and being hit with a saucepan'

It's A Funny Old World

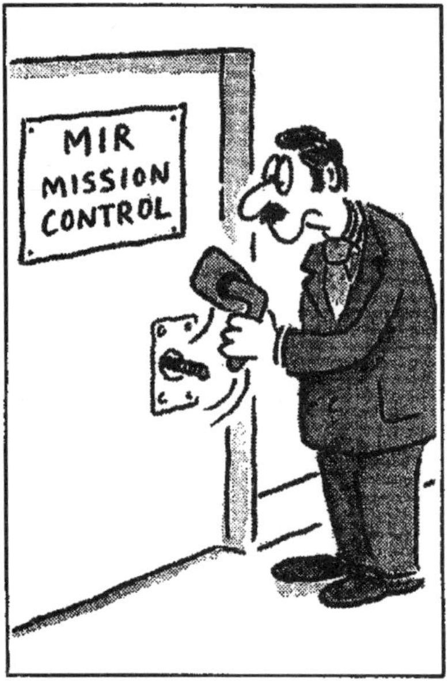
MIR
MISSION
CONTROL

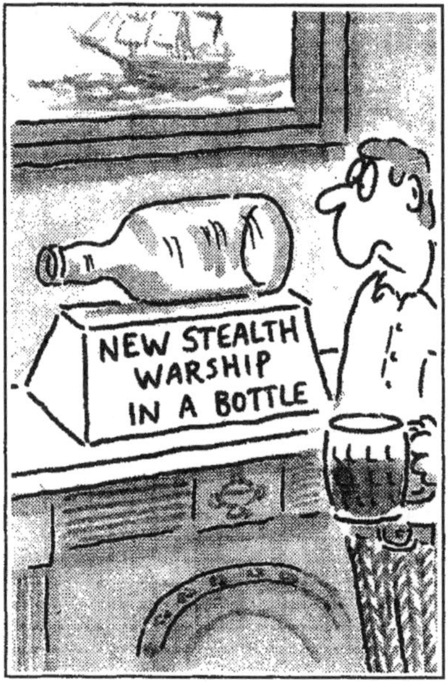
NEW STEALTH
WARSHIP
IN A BOTTLE

It's A Funny Old World

'Hey, a special stamp to commemorate the post strikes'

1998

The Sporting Life

'If you don't want to know
how your marriage ends,
look away now'

'At first it's all right and then
suddenly the ball appears in
the back of our goal'

The Sporting Life

'Wimbledon?
Follow that cloud'

The Sporting Life

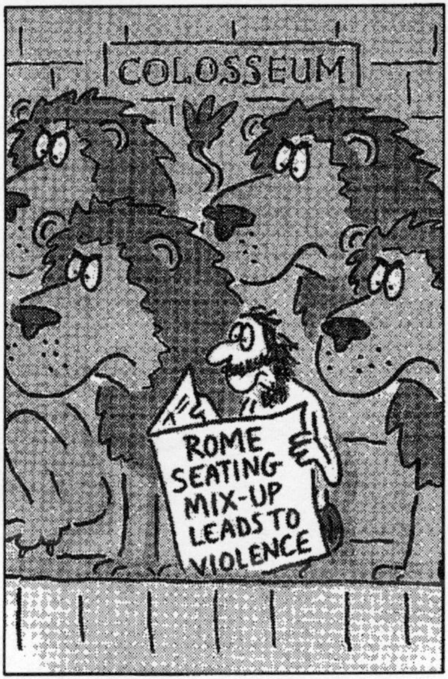
COLOSSEUM
ROME SEATING MIX-UP LEADS TO VIOLENCE

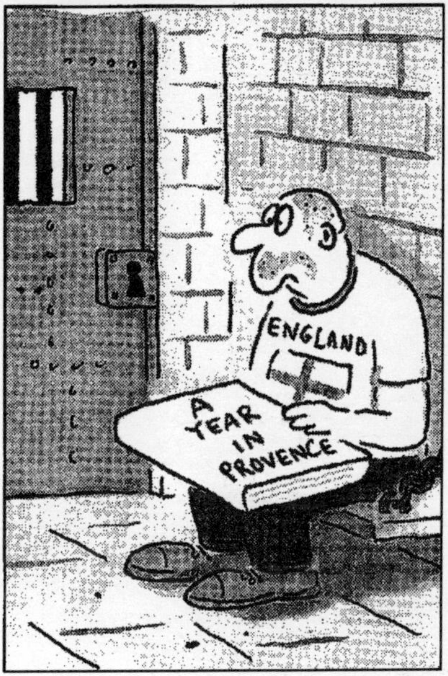
ENGLAND
A YEAR IN PROVENCE

Hard Times

'I'm worried it might crash when we go from BC to AD'

'Jump, Roberts - I want to see if you bounce back'

The Nation's Health

'They're the only thing left that is safe to eat'

'My compliments to the genetic engineer'

The Nation's Health

'I took a week off sick and, blow me, I fell ill!'

'We discovered Bovine Spongiform Encephalopathy in 1985, but it was two years before any of us could pronounce it'

The Nation's Health

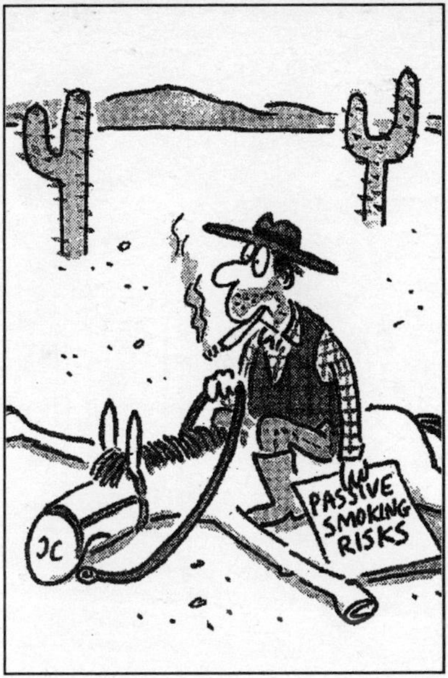
JC
PASSIVE SMOKING RISKS

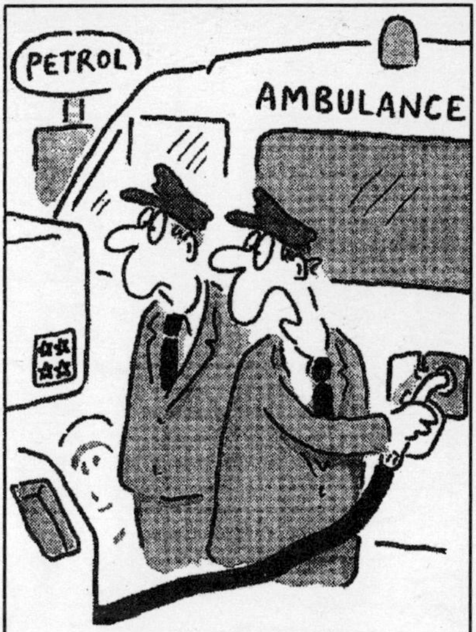
PETROL
AMBULANCE

'Well, that's used up the extra cash for the NHS'

Talking of Politics

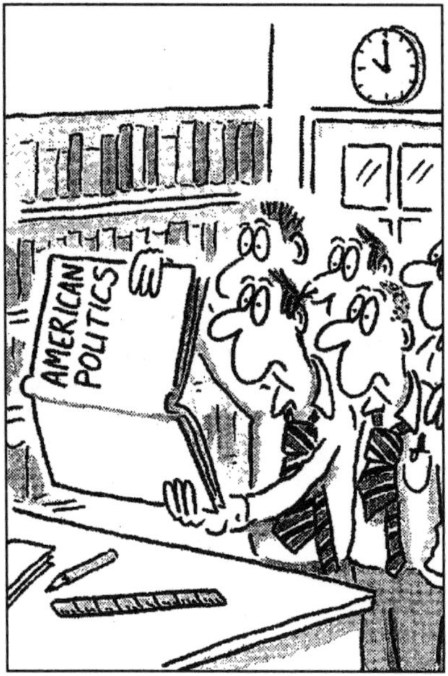
AMERICAN POLITICS

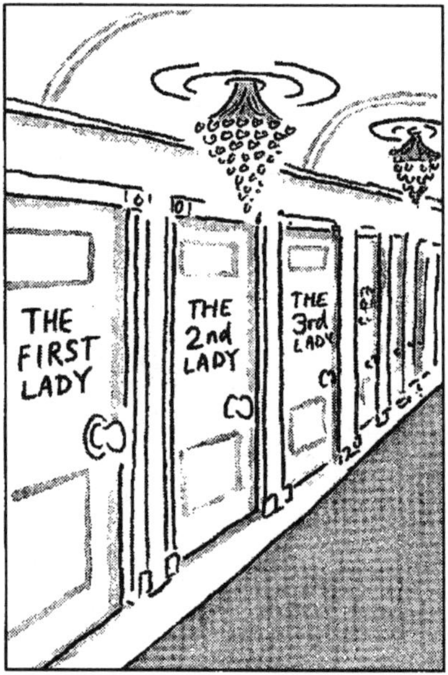
THE FIRST LADY
THE 2nd LADY
THE 3rd LADY

Talking of Politics

'I'll let you off this time, but remember this is meant to be Cool Britannia'

'Now it's turning really nasty - they're planting Leylandii trees along the border'

Transport Troubles

'The train left ten minutes ago — if you run you can catch it'

It's A Funny Old World

'My goodness, Rex, I had
no idea you were a Mason'

It's A Funny Old World

'Yes, sir, the bottled water was £300,000,000 because it came from the moon'

It's A Funny Old World

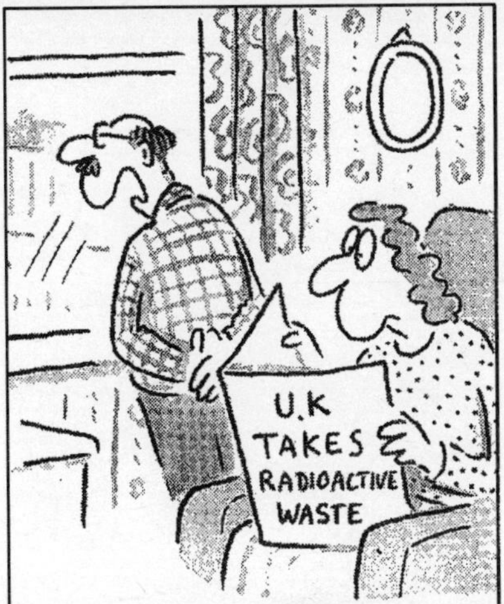

U.K TAKES RADIOACTIVE WASTE

'I wouldn't mind, only the dustmen won't even take my grass cuttings'

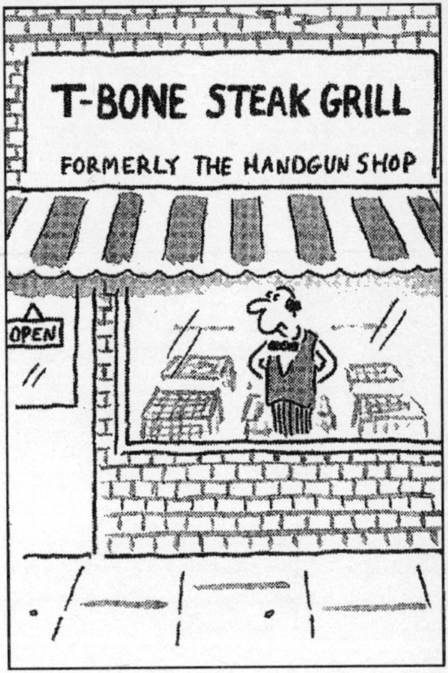

T-BONE STEAK GRILL
FORMERLY THE HANDGUN SHOP
OPEN

It's A Funny Old World

'Dad, I advise you
to do a runner'

'Please can you help me
work the video machine?'

It's A Funny Old World

'When I was your age we had to make our own accidents'

1999

Food Scares

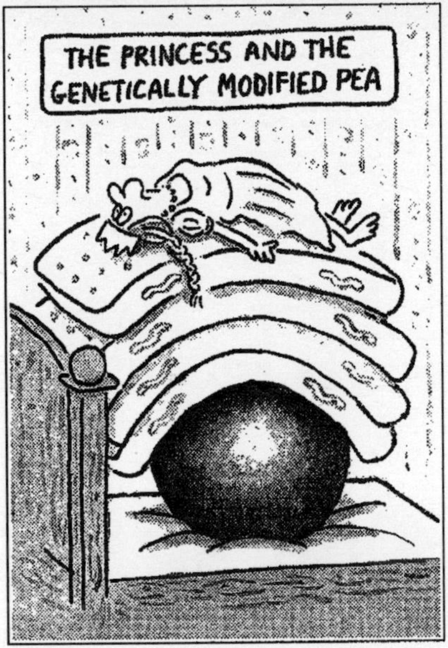
THE PRINCESS AND THE GENETICALLY MODIFIED PEA

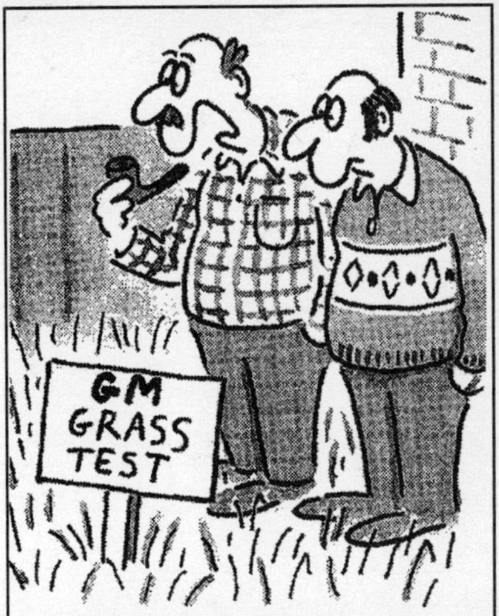
GM GRASS TEST

'It's not really, but I'm hoping Greenpeace will break in and mow it'

Food Scares

Mary had a little lamb
Its fleece was white as snow
She had to shoot it through
  the head
The lamb price fell so low

Food Scares

'Eat your vegetables or you'll never grow up to be big, strong and mildew resistant'

Law and Order

'You only stopped me because I'm green'

Law and Order

'In the old days we'd just get a clip round the ear'

'BUY YOUR OWN WATCH!'

Weather or Not

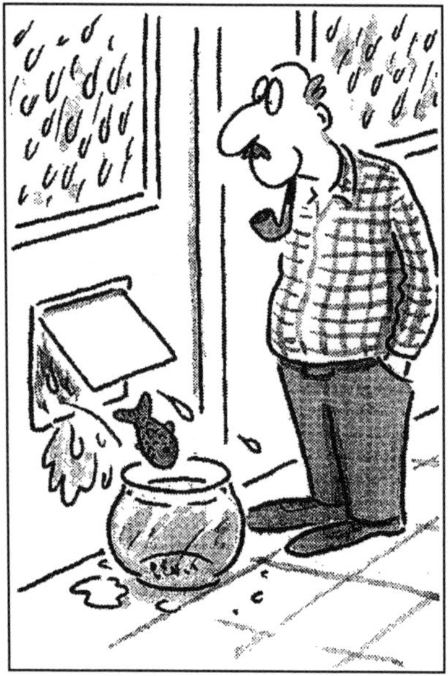

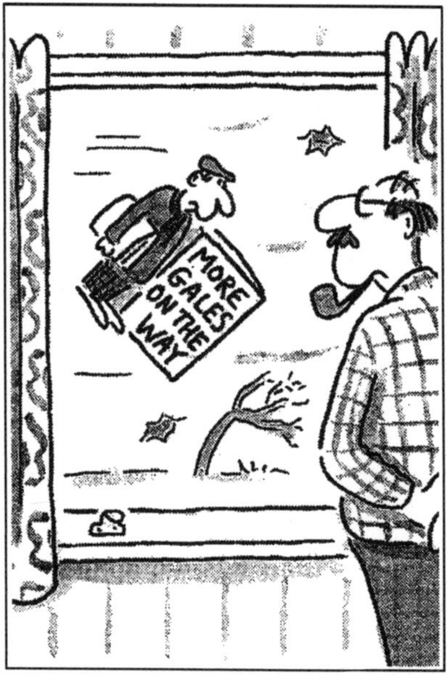
MORE GALES ON THE WAY

Talking of Politics

'Call up the Lewinsky-Clinton details but DON'T look'

'I've just discovered you're NOT an MI6 agent and you haven't been on a top secret mission'

Talking of Politics

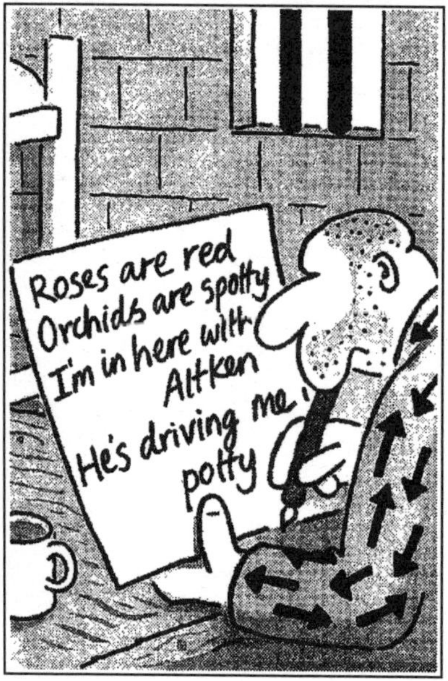
Roses are red
Orchids are spotty
I'm in here with
Aitken
He's driving me
potty

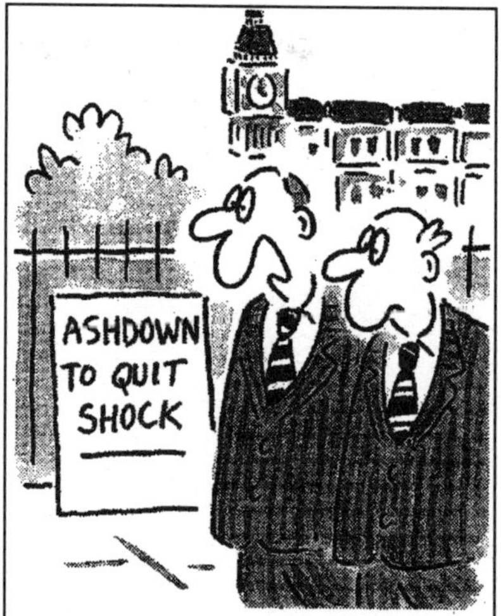
ASHDOWN
TO QUIT
SHOCK

'It's amazing, I've already forgotten where I was when I heard the news'

Talking of Politics

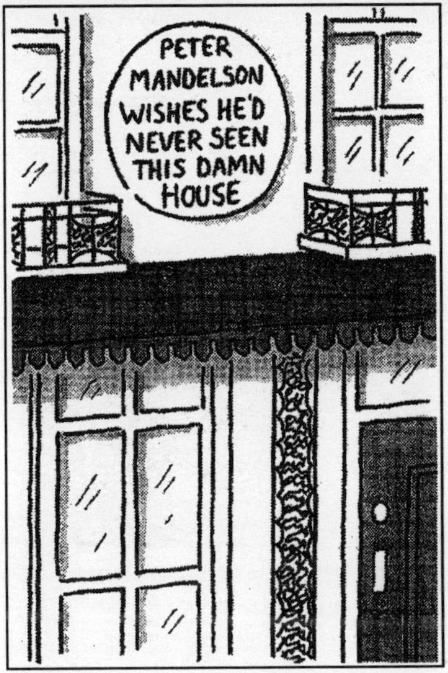
PETER MANDELSON WISHES HE'D NEVER SEEN THIS DAMN HOUSE

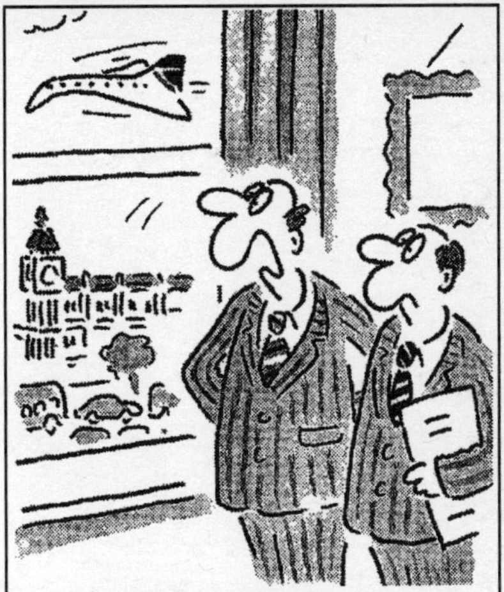

'Sometimes you can hear a distant boom as Jack Cunningham goes through the expenses barrier'

Talking of Politics

'I'm afraid you're on my list
of people who are not
allowed to speak'

'Darling, come out here
and watch the Euro
slowly going down'

Talking of Politics

'Does the Eurostar to Brussels
connect with the
EU Gravy Train?'

'Since Scottish devolution
he just does what he wants'

Lords Reform

'Their numbers have to be controlled and this is the most humane way'

'Isn't it time you were abolished, dear?'

The Modern Military

'I tried to get to the shops but cloud cover prevented me from reaching my target'

The Nation's Health

'It will all be worthwhile if it stops just one young person going into advertising'

'There, now I can't even find my cigarettes'

The Nation's Health

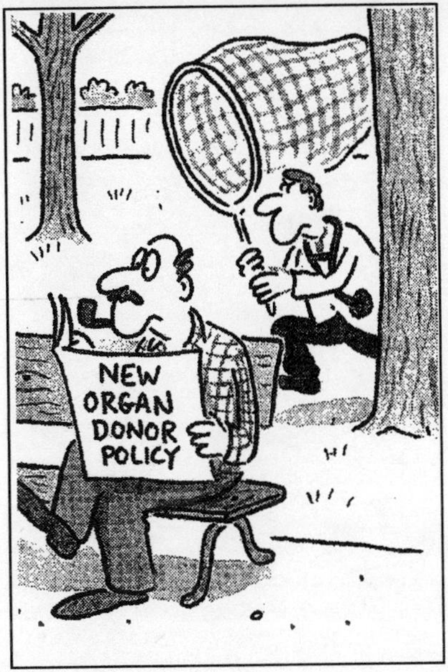
NEW
ORGAN
DONOR
POLICY

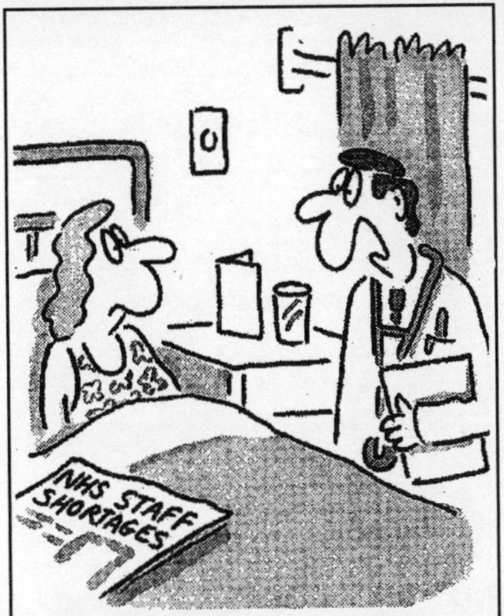
NHS STAFF
SHORTAGES

'By the way, while you were under anaesthetic you agreed to become a nurse'

The Sporting Life

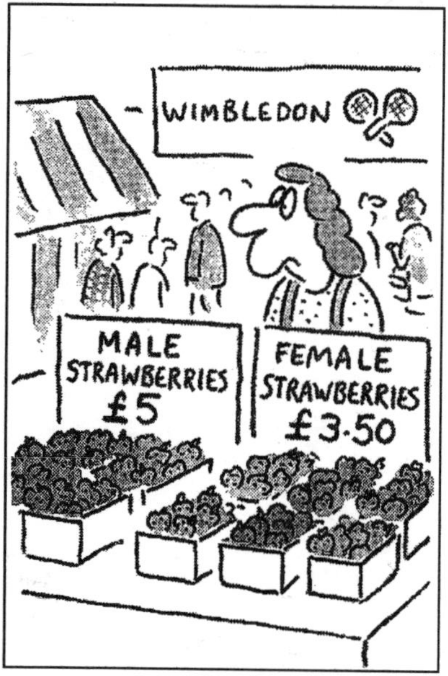
WIMBLEDON
MALE STRAWBERRIES £5
FEMALE STRAWBERRIES £3.50

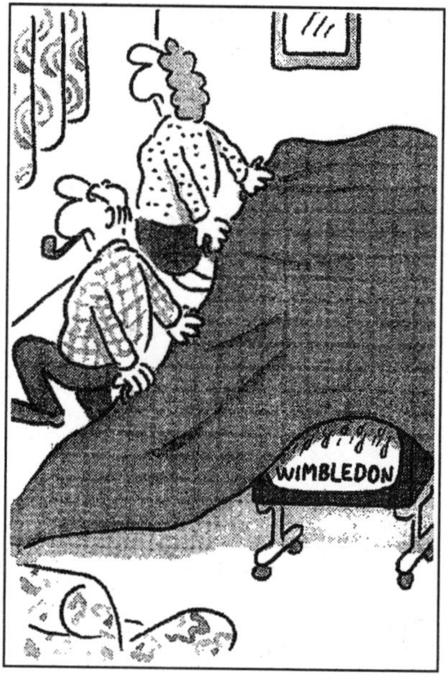
WIMBLEDON

It's A Funny Old World

'On a clear day you can see our car for £3,000 less than we paid for it'

It's A Funny Old World

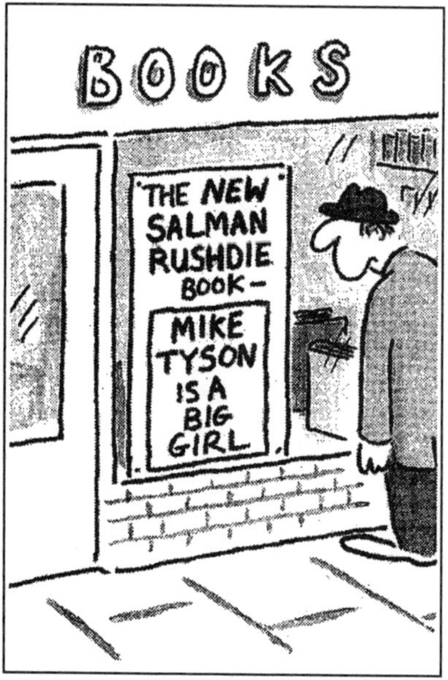
BOOKS
'THE NEW SALMAN RUSHDIE BOOK –
MIKE TYSON IS A BIG GIRL

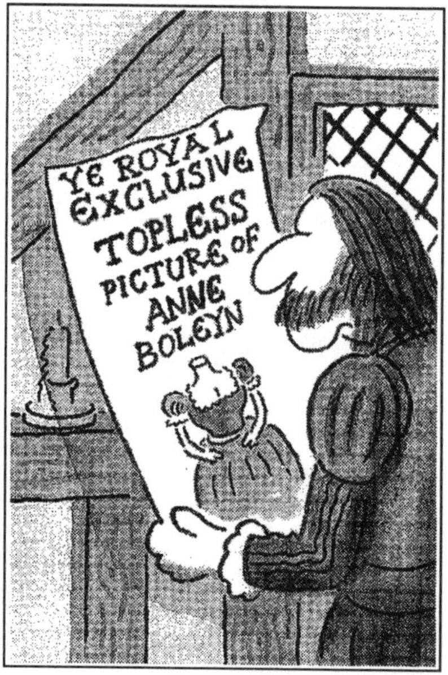
YE ROYAL EXCLUSIVE
TOPLESS PICTURE OF ANNE BOLEYN

It's A Funny Old World

'Same again?'

It's A Funny Old World

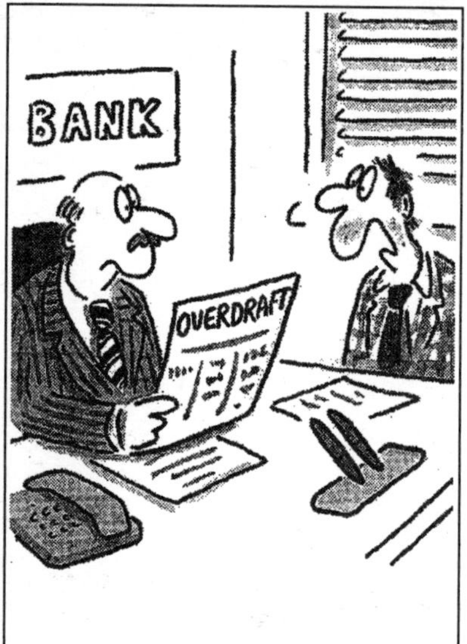
BANK
OVERDRAFT

'. . . . . . I might rally'

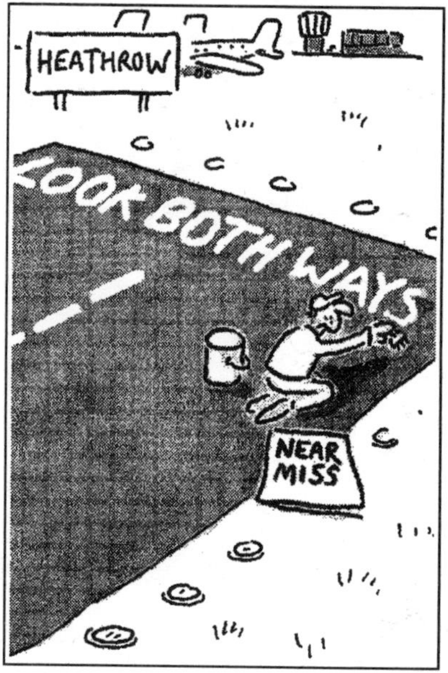
HEATHROW
LOOK BOTH WAYS
NEAR MISS

It's A Funny Old World

'There's talk of redundancies'

'Or, if you want something more expensive, I can show you this again tomorrow'

2000

The Countryside

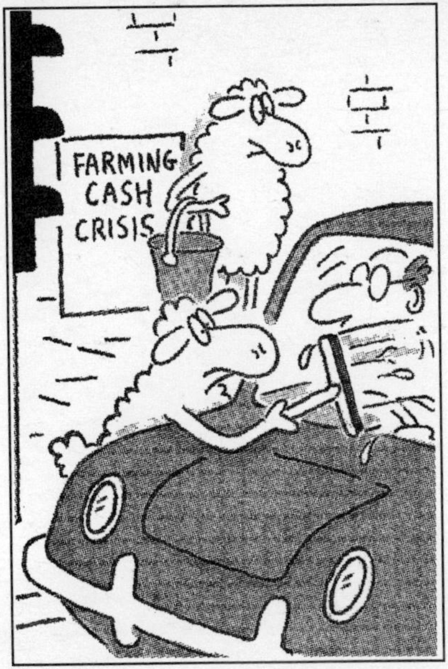
FARMING
CASH
CRISIS

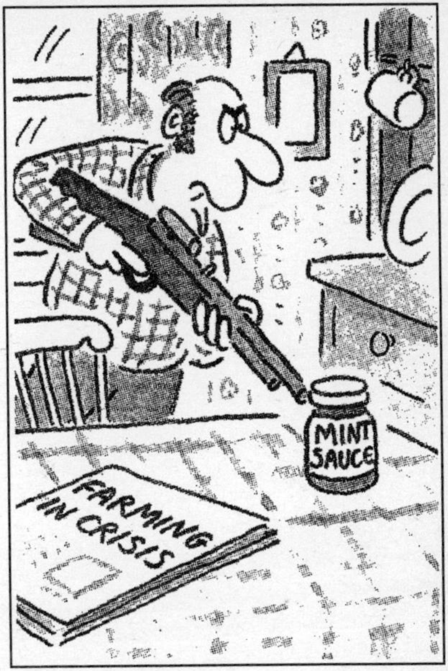
MINT
SAUCE
FARMING
IN CRISIS

The Countryside

'LOOK! A rural post office'

'Go past the derelict farm, turn right at the boarded-up post office and it's opposite the closed-down Barclays'

The Modern Military

'The only thing that stops me leaving is the fear that someone will kiss me goodbye'

'...And the Colonel gave me this one for having lovely eyes'

Motoring On

'For you, Tommy,
car production is over'

Motoring On

'You can have leather seats, air conditioning, and for a little extra, the whole company'

'It's cheaper than parking it'

Talking of Politics

'Be careful, it might lurch
to the right at any moment'

'As a gesture of protest I sent
Pinochet's luggage to Spain'

Talking of Politics

'I'm drinking to forget my PIN number'

'Oh no, the foxes have been at the dustbins again'

Talking of Politics

'Heckling the Prime Minister is one thing, but I don't agree with Cecily that we should blow up Hammersmith Bridge'

Talking of Politics

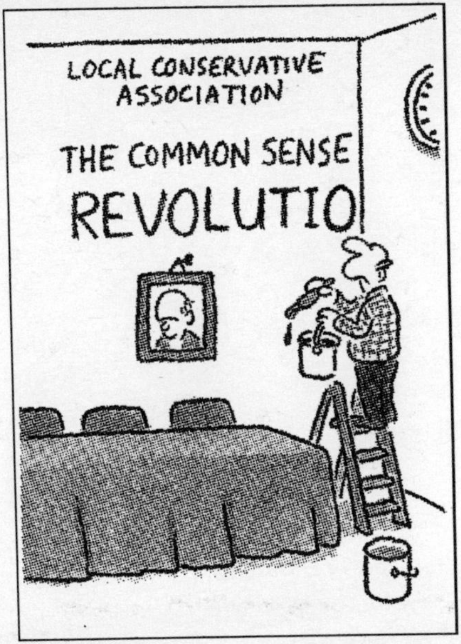
LOCAL CONSERVATIVE ASSOCIATION
THE COMMON SENSE
REVOLUTIO

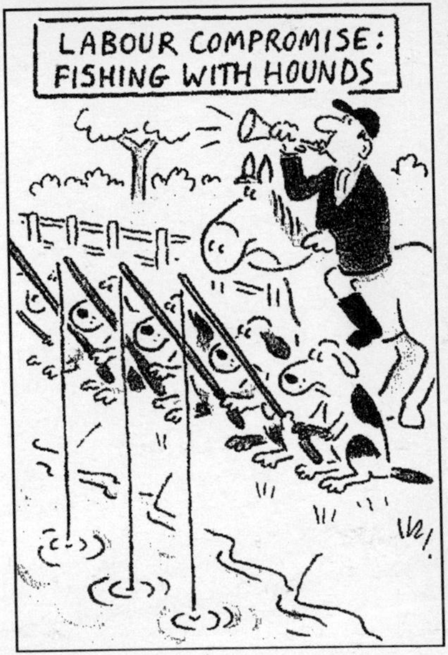
LABOUR COMPROMISE: FISHING WITH HOUNDS

The Nation's Health

'Say aarh...'

'He swallowed the
NHS questionnaire'

The Nation's Health

'You'd never believe the tales I could tell you about NHS waiting lists'

The Millennium

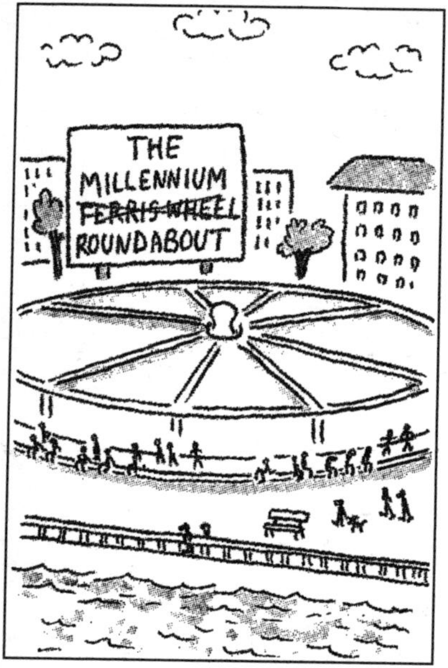
THE
MILLENNIUM
~~FERRIS WHEEL~~
ROUNDABOUT

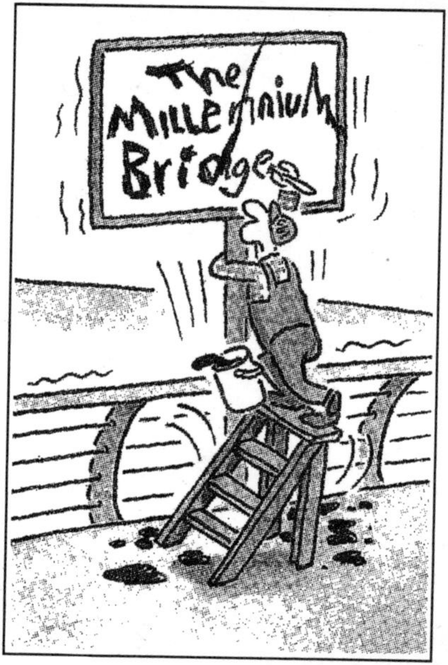
The
Millennium
Bridge

The Millennium

'Well, thank goodness our computer wasn't affected'

It's A Funny Old World

'The bookshop had sold out, so I stole this one from a child'

'Mum, Dad, come quickly – John Prescott is walking'

It's A Funny Old World

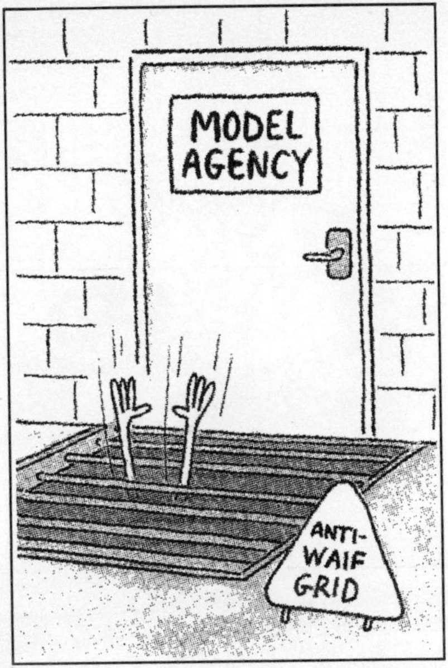
MODEL
AGENCY
ANTI-
WAIF
GRID

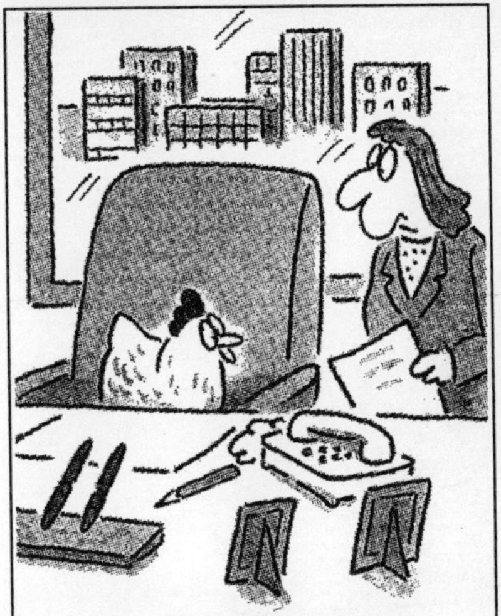

'I wanted to concentrate on my career, so I've had my eggs poached'

It's A Funny Old World

'I've come to take you to the Dunkirk anniversary celebrations'

'I said, WE'RE GOING TO BE HEARING THE PATTER OF TINY FEET!'

It's A Funny Old World

'Mowing the lawn
isn't "playing God"'

'Before the cat got its passport
it was always bringing
us back dead birds'

It's A Funny Old World

860,00C
NEW
HOMES

HOUSE PRICE CONVERSATIONS
UP AGAIN
MUCH
MORE
FREQUENT
BECOMING
TIRESOME
CAN
DOMINATE
DINNER
PARTIES
TALK OF
NOTHING
ELSE

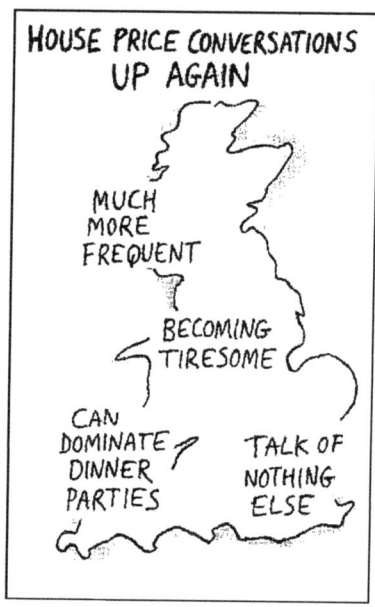